MW01596445

A Blueprint for

Rebuilding the "Church"

Reaching Those Who Have Become Marginalized In Our Traditional Mainline Denominations

Breaking Down Barriers
Building Bridges to The Cross

Rev. Stephen Crowell Mdiv

Pastor Craig Buelow

KonXions: A Blueprint for Rebuilding the "Church"

Editing by L.E. Capodagli

Printed in United States of America

Produced by Wave Dancer Productions

     P.O. Box 64
     Rushford, NY 14777

For further information concerning this topic please email Rev. Stephen Crowell @
pastor@konxions.org

"To live the gospel of Jesus Christ and to be God's love with our neighbors in all places."

(United Methodist Church Mission Statement 2011)

Table of Contents

Glossary of Terms

"KonXional DNA" – The Language of Connecting

Body of Believers or the Body of Christ – The Body of Christ are those who have committed their lives to Christ and have made Christ Lord of their life.

Circuit Riders – These are individuals that will mentor one or more KonXional Group Interpreters. They are in position to suggest Discovery Lessons for the KonXional Group. They are also instrumental in giving additional information to the Interpreters for the meetings. Circuit Riders will also answer questions that may come up in KonXional Groups. In most cases, Circuit Riders will be drawn from pastors who have completed seminary and have a passion for KonXional Groups. This position does not eliminate other pastors who have completed alternative educational requirements.

Core Requirements – Fellowship, Discipleship, Worship, Mission, and Evangelism

Core Theology – KonXions seeks to be relevant to a changing world. This relevancy neither promotes nor sanctions the concept that theological truths found in the Bible can change. KonXions identifies with eight foundational statements: we believe in a triune God; God created all that is seen and unseen; Jesus was both God and Man; God is still at work today through the Holy Spirit; the Bible contains all information for our Salvation; Jesus died and was resurrected for our salvation; there is a moral code of conduct; this moral code of conduct can be found in the Bible.

Covenantal Community – These are members of KonXional Group that commit themselves to each other for accountability and growth.

Discovery Lessons – In most cases Discovery Lesson will be produced on a DVD or stored on the KonXional website. The Discovery Lessons will be made available to all who view the website to maintain the philosophical statement that we need to break down barriers to the cross. These lessons will be produced by the KonXional Servants or purchased from locations that allow total access to their material without additional royalties.

Host – A person(s) who opens the home or place of business to members of the KonXional Group for planned meetings.

Interpreter – A person who has the responsibility in the KonXional Group to lead the discussion around the Discovery Lesson.

KonXional Groups – These small groups have agreed to follow five organizational points. They come together for fellowship, worship, discipleship, missional opportunities and evangelism. Each of these five points is not necessary at each event; however, Interpreters must be aware of their importance to form a comprehensive group.

Missional vs. Attraction Model – The Attraction Model is focused on bringing individuals to certain programs or personalities. The Missional Model is concerned with using one's talents and gifts to serve others. KonXions is all about service to those in the local community as well as the regions beyond.

Organic – This term refers to a healthy, living, growing body of tissue. It reproduces through a series of orderly, prescribed actions. It is believed that if KonXional Groups are healthy and following their missional mandate they will grow and produce more groups.

Outsiders – This is a term that is coined in the book "UnChristian." The author says that we can offend others when we call them sinners, backsliders, or other names that are negative in their connotation. It is felt at this time that "Outsiders" is a more correct term to use.

Relational – The overall mission of KonXions is to build relationships with each other and with those who are "Outside." Jesus commands us to Love God with all that we are, and we are to love others as we love ourselves. It is not about completing the lessons or the activities. These are merely pathways to relationships.

Regional Events – This area of ministry is extremely hard to categorize. These events are to be organized to meet a variety of needs. These events could range from seminars to tailgating at sporting events. These events could be the party after a motorcycle run or they could be simply a concert put on by those in a KonXional Group. These events are to also utilize the five points. Regional Events are to be free to all that participate.

Small Groups – Typically these groups range in size from three to twelve people. These groups come together for short determined periods of time to focus on a particular subject. Not all small groups are KonXional Groups.

Servant Leader – Servant leaders are those who have received the call and understand that all Christians are to perform acts of Priesthood. Servant Leaders understand that they are not volunteers. They are called to act out of obedience to Scriptural mandates.

Stewardship – All who follow after Christ are to follow the commands that were set forth through the teaching of Jesus and Scripture. KonXions believes that each member of a KonXional Group should fully participate in the celebration of giving through tithing ten percent of their income (or otherwise as directed by the Holy Spirit) and through giving of their time in Servant Leadership opportunities according to their spiritual and natural gifts. There is a cost associated with being an heir to God's Kingdom.

Volunteers Vs. Servants – Volunteers are individuals that believe they can pick and choose when to work for God. Servants are those individual that understand that they are commanded to answer God's call for their lives.

KonXions

Overview

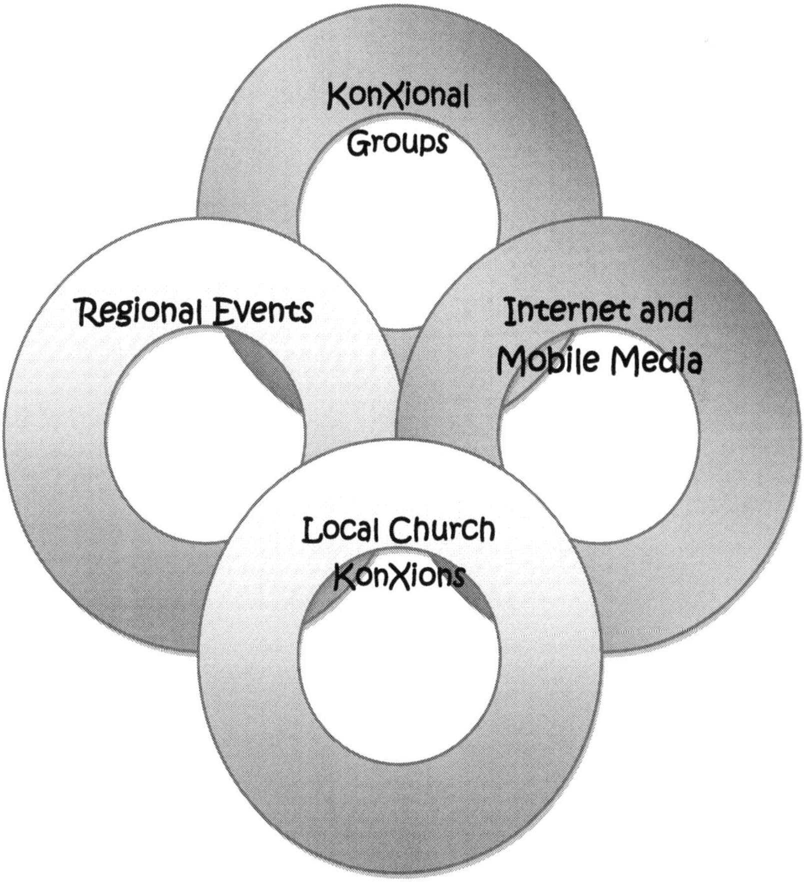

KonXional
Groups

Regional Events

Internet and
Mobile Media

Local Church
KonXions

The Ministry of KonXions

Why KonXions? (sounds like "connections")

KonXions is one of the solutions to the critical issue facing mainline traditional denominations. Congregants and members are disappearing and have been disappearing for a long time. The Call to Action Report (United Methodist Church), the Barna Group, Bishop Kim (Korean Methodist) and many others have publically voiced their concern. The time has come for radical involvement to stem this continuing loss of participation and the apparent apathy of those in the congregations. The methods used to reach out into the communities have simply not worked. The church has not changed their strategy to stay relevant with the younger population

Many authors, pastors and church leaders have attempted to look at and solve this problem. The United Methodist Church has invested $500,000 to understand the problems and potential solutions facing the church today in the "Call to Action Project." The one book that has offered a key to understanding the issue and ties all of the other books together is "UnChristian" by David Kinnaman.

In this book he mines the data collected by his team at the Barna Group to come to an understanding of why "Outsiders" no longer attend mainline churches. KonXions is tapping into all of these resources to develop a plan to reach those who have been marginalized or disenfranchised from the physical church setting. KonXions also reaches back into Methodist history to again utilize the power of small KonXional Groups that were formed by John and Charles Wesley.

What is KonXions?

Four major components comprise the ministry of KonXions. **KonXional Groups** are individual groups that meet regularly with three to twelve people. **Regional Events** provide an opportunity for the KonXional Groups to come together as the larger "Body of Christ." **KonXional Communications** will utilize the full power of the electronic world through the use of the internet and other mobile devices. **KonXional Union** stays connected with the local church by providing a new depth of relationships to the outside community that has become disenfranchised.

KonXions works to empower laity to become the leaders of these small KonXional Groups. It is within these groups that deep relationships can be built. Discipleship happens in a similar fashion as Jesus modeled. These small KonXional Groups meet in homes, parks, shops, restaurants, bars, and any other location that fits their individual needs. These groups allow for an extremely comfortable atmosphere where "outsiders" feel uninhibited in attending. This is one less barrier to overcome for those who are uncomfortable attending formal services.

KonXions seeks to use the missional model versus the attraction model. One of the key components for each of the KonXional groups is to find ways to get involved in the community as well as globally. The target audience must be involved both physically and emotionally to feel connected. Their generation is a generation of doing

KonXions Target Audience

KonXions seeks to reach those individuals, who range from eighteen into their early thirties, that are currently absent from the church setting. David Kinnaman makes the statement that those who are "Outside" have had contact with the church and with members of the church. They have been turned off from attending for many different reasons. Four major issues have been identified as the reasons for their departure: these individuals highly value relationships among their peers; they chose the family or "tribe" they want to become a part of and then become extremely loyal to this group; they have become disconnected from the church because the church setting does not give them a voice to express their opinions; and they need and want to take ownership of their ideas.

Missional Mandate

KonXions follows the mandate given by Jesus as he addressed his friends and relatives in the synagogue after his forty day retreat into the desert. Luke 4:18 & 19 (NRSV) "The Spirit of the Lord is upon me, because he has anointed me to bring good news to the poor. He has sent me to proclaim release to the captives and recovery of sight to the blind, to let the oppressed go free, to proclaim the year of the Lord's favor." Jesus confirmed this missional mandate to his disciples while in Jerusalem before his death. Jesus made it clear to them that they were to minister to others as if it were to Jesus himself. (Matthew 25:31-46.) Jesus modeled this mandate to show us how we were to live our lives.

KonXions is a ministry that seeks to reach out to those who need love, care, and a voice. KonXions follows the Great Commission where Jesus sent his disciples into the world to reach those who were outsiders and to disciple those who wish to grow into deep loving relationships with the triune God and with other people.

KonXions, a connectional small group ministry, seeks to meet the current needs found within our culture that prevent or inhibit the younger generations from becoming active members within the mainline traditional Church. KonXions mission is to find relevant models of ministry that will reach those that have been marginalized. KonXions believes that this mission is critical to complete the mission Jesus set for those who would follow after him.

KonXions seeks to follow the example that Jesus gave to us as he took twelve individuals aside for a period of time to disciple them in the truth found within God's Kingdom. It was through taking the time to be in fellowship with them that Jesus taught them about reaching out to others, meeting them at personal levels and sharing with the world the Good News. Jesus used teachable moments to worship God with the disciples. KonXions seeks to continue to follow the Wesley's model as they formed the Methodist movement.

KonXions will find creative ways in which people come together for fellowship and worship, to learn discipleship, to find missional opportunities and to reach others with the Good News.

Seeking to find
Relevance in Tradition

A Report on Why
KonXions is Vital
To the Church Today

Outdated Ideas

Rev. Slaughter's opening address at the Change the World '09 Conference raised several alarming issues. The traditional mainline church has been in a decline for over fifty years. Many different factors have allowed this phenomenon. The world in which we live is moving at lightning speed. Astronauts have visited the moon, countries that were once enemies are now trading partners, and traditional activities have become outdated. The church in general has not changed to stay relevant to the changing world around them. New wine skins are needed to reach those that have turned against the current traditional styles of worship and the church in general due to many different factors.

The traditional church has lost touch with the world which it has been raised to serve. This is because it has had a forward thinking mentality as its focus. This forward thinking does not have a true concern for the welfare of the lost. If asked, the church would almost certainly say that they do have a genuine concern for the lost, but their actions do not reveal it. David Kinnaman in "Un Christian" writes that outsiders think the people in the church are insincere. They will invite you to church, but are not seeking to develop true relationships.[1]

Some Christians have placed their hope in a future coming of glory when all true believers will be lifted up into Heaven. Because of this belief they have lost their focus on looking out for others, but seek only to concentrate on the "do's and don'ts" found in the Bible. Outsiders receive the message loud and clear from these Christians that they are more concerned about their lifestyle of doing it right than they are with relationships.

According to a poll taken by the Barna Group these Outsiders would be right. Two thirds of churchgoers believe in rigid rules and strict standards. "Three out of every five churchgoers in America feel that they "do not measure up to God's standards. And one-quarter admitted that they serve God out of a sense of "guilt and obligation" rather than "joy and gratitude."[2]

In another Barna poll, out of those who would call themselves Christian only nine percent believed all eight of the basic principles of Christianity. Out of ninety-five million Americans only three million would have a clear biblical worldview. These eight basics are: Jesus Christ lived a sinless life; the Creator of the universe is all powerful and all knowing; the Triune God rules still today;

---

[1] Kinnaman, David. 2007. Baker Books. Page 69 and others (see chapters 3 and 4

[2] Ibid. Page 51

the gift of salvation come from God and cannot be earned; Satan or the Devil is a real identity; Christians are called to share their faith in Christ with others; the Bible is accurate in the principals that are for the edification of the church; there are unchanging moral truths and these truths are found in the Bible.[3]

The church has not only lost touch with the world, but has lost touch with God's plan for the world. People in general may not know why they have left the church, but the church is losing people faster than they can rejuvenate. Every poll taken that surveys the attendance profiles will confirm that the average congregant is over sixty and the average attendance is less than fifty.

The church began to lose focus when it allowed itself to become trapped into a corporate model. Proponents of the "church growth" movement that became popular in the eighties and nineties structured themselves similar to large corporations. The pastor would have been considered to be the CEO with a board to help guide and steer their church. Rev. Slaughter illustrated the end result of this model. General Motors has lost sixty-three percent of the market shares to other manufactures that made cars that met the consumer needs. During this same time the United Methodists have lost fifty-one percent of their membership to entertainment and other activities that have better met their needs.

---

[3] Ibid. Page 75

Together we need to acknowledge that the traditional church is heading entirely in the wrong direction. Radical changes must be made quickly to avoid the impending disaster. One statistic that must change is the location of our worship centers. Seventy-nine percent of our churches are reaching only sixteen percent of the population.

The time has come for a radical change and a new model to emerge for Christians to be accountable to each other and to those "Outside." William Easum[4] in his book "Dancing with Dinosaurs" gives his reader a modern day parable to get a point across.

In Easum's story there was a woman who owned the finest winery in all of the land. In her winery were beautiful large wooden vats. These vats nurtured the crushed grapes until maturity. People came from all over the world to visit the winery that had been in the family for centuries. It was here that they produced the famous wine.

That was until one day when the wine developed a bitter taste. The women could not explain why, because she hadn't changed the process. She had continued on with

---

[4] Easum, William. Dancing with Dinosaurs. Abingdon Press. Nashville. 1993. Pages 11 & 12
This is an important book to have in ones library. Easum's books are prophet to how the church fails to move off from the tradition, while still giving hope for the church by giving insightful recommendations.

the centuries old traditions. Because the wine was now bitter both the visitors and the regular customers began to look for their wine elsewhere. Many consultants were brought in to find the problems. Each of them came to the same conclusion: the old vats were turning the crushed grapes sour. They concluded that the woman's only option was to replace the old vats, because they could not be cleaned.

The women who owned the winery could not give up her beautiful vats. They had been in her family for generations and were one of the foundations of the family's centuries-old tradition. She felt it was more important to keep the vats than it was to halt the declining number of customers coming to her winery.

She continued to make other attempts to improve her wine. She tried different fertilizers. She hired new grounds keepers who changed the acidity of the soil. She went so far in her desperation as to design new labels for the bottles. The one area in which she refused to budge was in getting rid of the old wooden vats. And so, the finest grapes in the world continued to produce bitter wine because they had to ferment in the old--but beautiful-- wooden vats.

It wasn't long after all of these attempts failed to see the day come when no one came to taste or buy the wine. Only faithful members of the family continued to drink the bitter product of stubbornness. It was more important for the family traditions to continue than it was to make satisfying wine.

This story speaks much of how the church is today. The church leaders are like the owner of the winery who knew why the grapes were making bitter wine. For years, each of our denominations has hired numerous consultants. Like the   owner of the winery, these church leaders have had all the knowledge they need to restore the church to its former glory.

But like the winery owner the church leaders and the church family have lacked the courage to use the knowledge at their disposal to make the changes necessary to produce satisfying wine like they had for years before. Unfortunately, church traditions run too deep to replace the "old vats". Churches live vicariously in stories of the glory days, with a hopeful belief that they will come again. The truth lies in front of them as their "world famous vineyards" fall into ruin, and it's only the stubborn family members that continue to "drink the bitter wine."

Hear Their Stories of Why They Left

The following stories are a small sample of those that I encountered in my search for those who have gone missing from our beloved traditional houses of worship. Unfortunately this entire book could have been filled with more stories of those who either walked away or felt they could never enter.

Janis is a single mom, who has attended church her entire life. In fact, her father was a pastor for many years. Janis grew up in the church and had served the church faithfully in worship, youth groups, Sunday School, on the Administration Board and in Vacation Bible School. Yet, she made the decision to pull out of church completely. I asked her to explain the burning question, "Why now?"

"I can't go back anymore. I am tired of people; it takes too much energy to go." Why? "Because, they are all hypocrites. They come to church and pretend to be something other than who they really are. But, it doesn't end there. I am the chief of the hypocrites. I pretend that I don't smoke and that I am not sleeping with my boyfriend. I can't tell them who I really am, so I have pretended to be this person that would be acceptable. If they knew the truth about me I would be shunned. I'm tired." Janis goes on to tell me that she still loves God and Jesus. But it hurts too much to be around those who have false expectations.

My own son, *Stephen*, grew up as a pastor's child. My wife and I had great intentions by sending him to youth meetings and other church functions. Unfortunately, that was where they taught him to smoke and drink. He hung out with church families that acted completely different during the week than on Sunday. Again, we thought if we sent Stephen to a private Christian boarding school he would see the right side of our faith. Instead, he saw the underside of our faith and he saw the inconsistency of the lives of his professors and those who lived in a 'religious town'. This totally turned him off from attending organized traditional churches.

Stephen ran as far away from his faith as he could possibly run. He went to Thailand where he could explore alternative religions. He came back seeing a commitment in the people there, not found here with the same sold out zeal. Fortunately, he has not been able to shake off his early training entirely. Ultimately he is still seeking a relationship with Christ to seal the deal for his salvation.

Still, he cannot get over the negative connotations that one word, "church." In fact, in his conversations with his friends they all mostly feel the same way. Just the word "church" causes them to literally "shiver." "Church"--it is a loaded word with many bad memories for many who have had similar bad experiences.

I met *Carl* once in a church setting and later in the hospital room where he was visiting a relative. Our true conversion started when his relative insisted that I needed to convince him to return to church. Pain shot across his face before he answered her request.

"Pastor, don't even try. I won't go back. It is not that I don't love God. I meet him in my own way. I pray all of the time and read the Bible. It is those people at church that I can't be around." I met with him later in private. He realized that he had habits that were looked down on from those who were "Holy." He wanted to live a life where he would not bend his integrity. He didn't want to fake it.

Returning to the Organic Truth of Scripture:
The Wesleyan Way

What of these stories? Can these people, and many others, be wrong in their thinking? Why are so many feeling this way? What are the feelings of the church and those members still in the church?

The traditional church has failed to recognize those outside of their walls are still wanting to be connected to their God. Therefore, I envision creating a new ministry within the body of the mainline Church called KonXions. It is through this ministry that we will seek to break barriers that have held people back from becoming a part of the worshiping body of God. KonXions seeks to reclaim the vitality of the early church found in the gospels, Acts and the early epistles. The body of Christ is found in community. We saw this come alive in the ministry of our founding fathers, John and Charles Wesley. They saw that the Anglican Church was not reaching large numbers of people. So, John and Charles Wesley sought to bring Christ and his message back to the common man. The firestorm spread across England, Ireland, Scotland, and then it jumped across the sea to the colonies.

Space is More Than Bricks and Mortar:

The Historical Scriptural Model

> *"On small groups - This is where people, meeting in small groups, will experience the feeling of family, an experience which will feed them into the worship of the larger body. Public worship is a corporate action. If you don't know anyone and you feel as though you are among a group of strangers, your worship will not be as free and expressive as it could be if you feel the warmth, the acceptance, the support of a family group."[5]*

I believe that Robert Webber gets it right in the quote above. The Holy Scriptures reveal to the reader that small groups became the normative model to follow. Jesus began his ministry with breaking from the model of where people should meet with Yahweh that was set in place by Moses. First, the Hebrews met their God, Yahweh, in the wilderness in the Tabernacle. The Tabernacle and the inner court area was the center of their camp.

Each day they were reminded of whom they served by simple physical placement of the Tabernacle. The

---

[5]Webber, Robert E. 1996. Blended Worship. Hendrickson Publishers. Page 79

location of their tents around the Tabernacle also reminded them of the community that was built by their relationship with the other tribes. King David laid the foundational work for the building of the first Temple. It was in King Solomon's Temple that Yahweh established a permanent residence among the chosen people. Regional synagogues were developed for worship for those who could not travel to the temple. These synagogues became the constant reminder of the God they served. It was in one of these very synagogues that Jesus begins his small group ministry.

Luke 4:14-21, 28-31 (NRSV) Then Jesus, filled with the power of the Spirit, returned to Galilee, and a report about him spread through all the surrounding country. He began to teach in their synagogues and was praised by everyone. When he came to Nazareth, where he had been brought up, he went to the synagogue on the sabbath day, as was his custom. He stood up to read, and the scroll of the prophet Isaiah was given to him. He unrolled the scroll and found the place where it was written: "The Spirit of the Lord is upon me, because he has anointed me to bring good news to the poor. He has sent me to proclaim release to the captives and recovery of sight to the blind, to let the oppressed go free, to proclaim the year of the Lord's favor." And he rolled up the scroll, gave it back to the attendant, and sat down. The eyes of all in the synagogue were fixed on him. Then he began to say to them, "Today this scripture has been fulfilled in your hearing." When they heard this, all in the synagogue were filled with rage. They got up, drove him out of the town, and led him to the brow of the hill on which their town was built, so that they might hurl him off the cliff. But he passed through the midst of them and went on his way. He went down to Capernaum, a city in Galilee, and was teaching them on the Sabbath.

Scripture reveals to us that Jesus met with and taught larger groups of people in synagogues. KonXional Regional Events serve the same purpose in reaching and teaching large groups today. Yet, there are a significant amount of stories that relate to Jesus' ministry to the people in remote areas. He took the time to meet with the large crowds of people. But, it was in the quiet times that he met with his twelve disciples. It was there that he taught them the principles found in the Kingdom of Heaven.

> *Luke 5:1-3 (NRSV) Once while Jesus was standing beside the lake of Gennesaret, and the crowd was pressing in on him to hear the word of God, he saw two boats there at the shore of the lake; the fishermen had gone out of them and were washing their nets. He got into one of the boats, the one belonging to Simon, and asked him to put out a little way from the shore. Then he sat down and taught the crowds from the boat.*

Peter and Paul continued to follow Jesus' example. They began their ministry teaching and/or participating in the Temple or synagogue. The Jews, who worshiped in the Temple or synagogues, did not appreciate the messages being preached by the Apostles. Eventually, the scriptures in Acts show the development of the home church. Acts chapter two explains that the believers came together to break bread and to devote themselves to the teaching of the Apostles.

Further evidence of house churches can be found in the letters of Paul to the small communities of believers he established wherever he traveled and ministered. Even though these communities were small enough to meet in homes they were not without their problems. We see this in I Corinthians. Paul becomes aware of a problem within the house church concerning the Eucharist.

The establishment of church buildings did not become popular until the reign of the Roman Emperor, Constantine. Church structures were built to mirror or imitate the temples serving state authorized gods. These churches were an incentive for non-believers to worship in structures that they were used too.

KonXions, an emerging church movement within the traditional Church, embraces Robert Webber's theory that the small group model is the most effective way to reach and disciple people who have become strangers with the local traditional church. Even though the trappings are the same as found in the Hebrew's wilderness encampment, many people in today's society refuse to recognize the church with the steeple in the middle of town as the center of their spiritual life.

Rev. Slaughter also sees this as a problem. "Our society is marked by increased spiritual hunger and activity, yet overall attendance in churches has decreased. The number of people in attendance weekly in United Methodist churches has been declining for years – dramatically so."[6] The total number of people turned off from attending organized worship on any given weekend is about three quarters of Americans[7] and the number of Canadians is even higher.[8]

It is time for the church to return to its spiritual roots and to rediscover the organizational genius of the Wesley brothers. Just as the Wesley's met in small groups they also held large outdoor events to reach the masses. It is time to reestablish small groups based not in churches, but in individual homes or wherever people congregate.

Developing a New Brick and Mortar Model

The Traditional Model

The structures that we call church have been established for the purpose of gathering in one place the

---

[6] Slaughter, Michael. 2002. Unlearning Church. Abington Press. Nashville. Page 19

[7] Hadaway, Kirk, Penny Long Marier, and Mark Chaves." What the Polls Don't Show". American Sociological Review, vol. 58, no. 6 (6 December, 1993), 741-52

[8] Bibby, Reginald. 1995. There's Got be be More: Connecting Churches and Canadians. Winfield Books, BC: Wood Lake Books. Page 16

people who call God their Savior and Lord of their life. Over the ages these churches and cathedrals have taken on a life of their own. They not only occupied a physical space, but have created an emotional and spiritual space where people have come expecting to meet God. Unfortunately for some, these spaces have become the equivalent of God. If you don't believe me, go into any church that has a history longer than fifty years and begin to remove or even move articles from the building. If the pastor is daring and takes on the challenge to move items around it doesn't take very long to find most of the sacred cows.

I was one of those pastors. Early in my career I learned of this truth and learned my lesson quite quickly in the Leon Wesleyan church (now closed). The church had been shepherd by the late Reverend Geneva Pritchard. She became synonymous with the church. She purchased the "throne" chairs and most of the other fixtures. She even bought the rug that lay just inside the entry doors. After several years of being there I saw that the rug was in dire need of being washed. I took it home and failed to get it back in time for the Sunday services. I was met at the door of the church and read the riot act for removing the rug and ordered to return it before the service started.

The Church has become a Sacred Place

The following quote establishes an argument for the division between the people established in the church model and those who work and play in the shadow of the church steeple. "Sacralization in emerging churches is about one thing: the destruction of the sacred/secular split of modernity. The modern period was characterized by the birth of the idea of secular space, that is, the idea of a realm without God. Before this time, in every culture, all arenas of life were spiritual; it was impossible to label some practices "religious" and others not."[9]

The concept of creating different space that was formed during the Modernity period created a rift between the church and life in general. The sanctity of life was now compartmentalized. "The marginalization of religious practice continued until the 1960's when many of the Western presuppositions about reality began to be deconstructed within the culture. Questions about Western superiority and "progress" began to be raised. A desire for a spirituality that embraced all of life began to be resurrected."[10] The emerging church is about giving all of life a sense of sacredness. The bottom line is about giving back to God all of life through worship and to recognize God is in all things and activities.

Creating New Space where all is Sacred

KonXions seeks to break down all barriers to the cross of Jesus. New spaces must be found that will

---

[9]Gibbs, Eddie & Ryan K. Bolger. 2005. Emerging Churches. Baker Academic. Grand Rapids. Page 66
[10]Ibid. Page 66

encourage those outside the walls to participate. Two couples who own *In the Blood and Piercing*, a tattoo parlor located on the south side of Pittsburgh, are deeply committed to Christ and to sharing their belief in him. Because of the love they show to others their parlor has become a hangout for recovering alcoholics, working people in the neighborhood, college students, single moms and social iconic outcasts with colored spiky hair.[11]

One young man attended church all of his life, but finally decided it wasn't worth it anymore since he didn't receive any spiritual enlightenment. He couldn't sit still and listen because of his Attention Deficit Disorder. So, one Sunday he decided to go waterskiing. He took a friend along with him for company and to drive the boat. Before they launched the boat he decided to pray. He asked his non-believing friend, who was caught off guard, if he had any prayer requests and then proceeded to pray. He also took the time to read a short section in the Bible. It didn't take long before he was witnessing to the entire boating community.

Jess Moody in "A Drink at Joel's Place" says that the church is upset because the world won't sit up and take notice of them. He turns it back around and says the church needs to understand that the world isn't under any

---

[11] Frost, Michael, 2006. Exiles. Hendrickson Publisher's. Peabody, Mass. Page 61

obligation to pay it any attention. The church must earn the right to be heard.

Moody claims that the fellowship is better in other spaces than in the church setting. He compares a bartender to a preacher and wonders which one is a better listener. Uptight church members complain that a person would even consider going into a bar. But to the outsider they enter in knowing that they will not be judged for all the things that they do wrong. The other reason for going into the bar is to have a little bit of fun.

Most Christians will agree that church is very rarely a place for enjoyment. The church must find ways to reestablish a connection to the world to begin to show the world Christ's love.[12] Moody equates the small group setting as a space where people can find fellowship. Finding these different spaces to meet with others is part of the unique mission KonXions sets out to accomplish.

Small Group Spaces

KonXions mission in developing the small group space is to bring all people into a relationship with the Trinitarian God, with others they come in contact with, with others that they share common ground, and with the created world in which we live. The term KonXions is based on the premise that all of creation was formed with the need to be in relationships. Thus, the first part of the

---

[12] Moody, Jess. 1967. Word Books. Waco, Texas. Pages 17-19

name stems from Koiniona, a word used in scripture meaning those in close fellowship; family, for instance. The large X stands for placing Christ in the center of our lives and also into the center of our ministry. KonXions realizes that it is essential to develop points of contact that will attract people to come into fellowship with the body of believers and with the Trinitarian God.

Loneliness in America has reached epidemic proportions. In part, we believe it is because we have lost the art of sitting out on the front porch after dinner. That was where our parents or grandparents would talk to the neighbors and to those who happened by. Instead we now sit inside watching other people act out the dramas that were once part of our daily stories.

Jesus the radical change agent becomes our model in creating points of hospitality. Isn't it interesting that Jesus can be seen "eating his way" through the gospels? It seems that he would eat with anyone that would sit down with him long enough. Tax collectors, prostitutes, fishermen, and even religious leaders found that Jesus would share a meal with them. Food has a way of bringing people together from all walks of life. The house churches in the book of Acts built their meetings around the common meal followed by the Eucharist (communion).

KonXions seeks to incorporate many different cultural avenues beyond the intimate small groups that meet in people's homes, bars, restaurants, parks or wherever the group decides. KonXions can be seen as four connected circles. Each circle is a point of entry and also a point of being connected with the larger body. Small groups form the **foundation where relationships are built** through both the meal and a worship experience.

The second point of contact and education is an interactive website that provides a place for community discussion, Bible studies, archives of past lessons and Bible studies, announcements, and postings for missional servant ministry.

Another circle of relationship building and spiritual growth is provided through missional opportunities. I, Stephen, have been on several missional trips. I find it most intriguing that we are ministered to more than those we went to give some sort of aid. Recently, I returned from a trip where we truly made an impact on those we helped. Yet, in my office talking with one of the men that went with me was telling me that God was working in his life in a mysterious way. He was now feeling more connected with others and especially with those he went with on the trip.

Regional Celebration Events meet monthly. One example of a Regional Event could on a Friday night with a seeker-friendly experience complete with music, stage lighting, food, dancing and a brief message. Another Regional Event could be a Saturday morning that begins with an opening rally, and then several breakout W.I.R.E.D seminars (Working In Religious Education).

Contemporary services need to develop a "climate" or "feel" that is relaxed and accepting in an environment that is conveying a "come as you are" atmosphere. It is important to emphasize the relational and lean more to the informal. Note that informal does not give license to becoming sloppy or unplanned. Contemporary worship that is done well breaks down barriers through a warm, inviting climate. The surrounding culture may give clues to on how to create an informal service. We are leaning that people value acceptance and warmth where they can carry their life's baggage into group setting and be welcomed. KonXions, through the small group setting, creates an environment of close fellowship where one could bring the dirty laundry of their lives and be accepted. The new brick and mortar model finds spaces that build on people's relational experiences.

People become the brick and the experience becomes the mortar.

Settings Still Matter

Robert E. Webber (a professor of Theology at Wheaton College since 1968) was visiting Moscow, one of the largest cities in the world. On this one particular Sunday he attended the Church of the Holy Trinity. Upon entering he immediately was crushed in the shoulder to shoulder crowd worshiping there. The people were packed from the front all the way back to the large wooden doors. Since there are no pews in the Orthodox churches in Russia the people were all standing. Dr. Webber was greeted by a woman who spoke through a translator. Upon learning that he was an American Christian she was overwhelmed with joy. She pulled Dr. Webber along behind her as she pushed her way through the crowded multi-domed cathedral.

It was here that he was able to fully appreciate the emotion-filled worshipers. They were all being transported to a heaven that was in their midst. They were lost in participation that included lifting not only their faces heavenward but also their hands and their prayers. Their own singing seemed to be that of hosts of angels, cherubim and seraphim. He began to realize that in the intellectualized American worship seldom did he ever see these signs of worship: closed eyes, tears, and very expressive hands. Yet, here they were together, old and young alike expressing emotion through wonder and praise.

Dr. Webber began to look around at his surroundings. The walls and ceilings were covered in various icons and frescoes. The walls hosted the entire company of the saints. The domed ceiling had Christ ruling over the heaven with chosen saints like Abraham, Moses, David and the twelve apostles. He began to feel drawn into the realm of the heavenly company of saints. "This was a pivotal experience for me: it left me very aware of the importance of the environment in which we worship, a matter to which all renewing congregations must attend."[13]

KonXions seeks to pay close attention to the details concerning the environment during each of The Events. The design team will work ahead of each major event to ensure that the setting provides an array of iconic images to be displayed in print or on large screens. When the small groups gather decorations can be added to help enhance the worship experience.

Safe Places

The world in which we live has changed--or so we believe. The only difference is that we have become aware of humanities sinful nature. Unfortunately for the Catholic Church they have to publicly deal with the issue of

---

[13]Webber. 1996. Blended Worship. Hendrickson Publishers Pages 99 - 102

children's (congregant's) safety in the public arena. The church had always been considered to be a safe place for people to come and find rest. Unfortunately all churches are filled with humans that have been affected by original sin. Imperfect people live and worship within the walls of the church. The challenge for those in leadership is to first recognize that there are potential dangers lurking around each closed door or in those cars that transport people.

Sadly, though, abuse within the church is done not only to children, but inflicted on people from all ages and backgrounds. Power is given over to those with authority. This power can be abused by ministers, congregational leaders, teachers and even the stranger to the church. On the other side of the coin the news stations bring us stories of people who become upset with the church and enter a worship session to inflict pain and suffering with their guns.

KonXions mission is to create places that are safe for all to attend. The United Methodist Church has produced literature (*Safe Sanctuaries)* and policies to protect those who come to worship. The church has realized that people need to feel safe so that they can become truly vulnerable to the message of the Lord.

KonXions desires to create these spaces in the homes, parks, curbsides and all places that our congregants and guests will meet. To accomplish this, the leadership of KonXions will review the policy of the United Methodist Church and other denominations to develop a workable

Safe Event Policy. This Policy will be set in place and enforced with all leaders.

KonXions will create a task force that will review each of the situations that we will enter to create the best possible experience. Child care will be provided as necessary with individuals who have been completely vetted. Background checks will be performed on all leaders.

The small group setting provides KonXions with the most challenging situations. We encourage the groups to allow the children to fully participate in the meetings when age and subject matter appropriate. KonXions ministry team could also develop activities that will focus on keeping them involved during the meeting. This idea fulfills the mission of breaking down all barriers to the cross, including age. Children should have equal access and also lead us in our worship.

KonXions recognizes that "church space" has become more than just the traditional four walls where people walk in the shadow of a steeple. "Church space" now includes any area where two or more meet together in the name of the Lord Jesus Christ.

Liturgy is Still Vital

"Truth is not simply a set of abstract ideas; it walks and talks. We hear the truth as we hear about what God is doing concretely in people's lives. Post-modern people understand reality in multiple ways. There is more than one way to do things, more than one thing going on at a time, and more than one message coming across. Building on that idea, narrative is key. Who wants to listen to abstract, context-less propositions when one can hear or watch a story unfold?"[14] The "catholic" or universal church has had to struggle with the concept of presenting the truth of God from the beginning of creation. Those who walked in the desert learned not from a written word, but from stories that had been handed down over time. The prophets many times used visual illustrations to get the point across. The prophet Hosea lived his train wreck of a marriage out in front of those he was called to minister to.

The Liturgy of Worship has developed or adapted with each passing era. Each of these changes in worship style has occurred with an onslaught of in-house fighting. Constantine began pulling the segregated church together with a Council of the Bishops creating a common creed that the entire empire could unify under. Armies were created

---

[14]Gibbs, Eddie & Ryan K. Bolger. 2005. Emerging Churches. Baker
   Academic. Grand Rapids. Page 68

to hold worshipers under the control of the church. Christian martyrs were burned at the stake because they dared to promote a change with the system of worship.

How a person chooses to worship is to be taken seriously. It is not the purpose of this book to change the manner in which many people find God through their weekly journey into the inner sanctum of a prescribed place of worship with a predetermined format. The act of change normally has been to create new systems that are mandatory for those currently worshiping in a chosen style. Those people are then expected to change to accommodate the needs and desires of others. This act within a church body normally causes friction between those who want change and those who wish to keep things status quo. It is my belief that a new system of worship style should be created to partner with existing sister churches to provide alternatives.

Society as a whole has moved on from current church methodologies. Evidence of this is found within the falling attendance records. Church congregants have aged. The medical system has put the traditional church into a life support mode by extending the average life span. Methodologies must change to attract those who have been left behind and marginalized by the traditional church. The message of the Good News is transcendent from its earliest message given in the garden. Jesus, through his teaching, dramatically changes the landscape of worship, both in method and intended recipient.

KonXions understands that liturgy is merely a form of presenting the Good News. KonXions has at its disposal many new and different forms in which to spread this Good News. At a recent Event we used Dog the Bounty Hunter in a video montage to promote his theme that we all are second chance people. This video was supplemented with several songs that made the same point. Pastor Craig and I shared our testimonies in which we expressed how we were "Second Chance People."

Music, Literature, and Film

Scripture introduces the reader to different passages that show the importance of music in the life of the worshiper. King David soothed the troubled soul of Saul and later wrote music to convey his expressions of worship. We are allowed to see the end results of David's hymns and prayers in the book of Psalms. Churches around the world continue to use these songs in modern day musical settings in their Hymnal. Music has been part of the organized church ever since.

Charles Wesley recognized that the Anglican Church was not meeting the needs of those who were being marginalized by those in the higher social stratum. Charles realized that the music in the church did not resonate with the common person. Factory workers and common laborers did not worship in the church settings, in part, because of the "high liturgical" settings.

Charles followed after his friend, Rev. Whitfield, and began to preach to the common person in the streets and in the fields. Charles and John Wesley transformed music when their poems were set to culturally relevant tavern music. They used the music that was popular with the people they were ministering to. This may come as a surprise to many congregants today who sit in their pew complaining about the new contemporary music.

Emerging churches are rediscovering the need to reach those who are again being marginalized by the church. Traditional mainline churches have remained stagnated with hymns that range in age from Calvin to the early 1900's. Only occasionally do new songs find their way into the hymnals.

The mega-church has replaced the streets and fields used by the Wesleys. Large crowds flock to these churches that have begun to break with the traditional worship models by incorporating contemporary Christian music and lights to recreate popular entertainment venues. "Willow Creek makes it known that they do not worship on Sunday. It is a time for evangelism using created music, drama, and arts to communicate the gospel message. Some fifteen thousand come to gather at this "seeker-friendly service." They come together on Wednesday and Thursday for their believers worship services."[15]

The mega-church movement began to break the

---

[15]Webber, Robert E. 1996. Blended Worship. Hendrickson Publishers. Page73

mold on how churches should look and act. New churches are beginning to spring up that intentionally target those who do not attend the traditional church. These churches are seeing the need to use all forms of media to get their point across. This trend has spurred mainline churches to add multi-media formats to retain those who are attracted to alternative forms of experiencing music.

KonXions Opens the Door Wide to All Music

KonXions understands that people from all walks of life experience music differently from each other. Battle lines have been drawn in the sand all across Canada and America concerning the music that is played in church. The music didn't change for generations and long traditions were well established because of this. Favorite hymns could be sung without even glancing down at the hymnal. These songs became virtual family traditions passed down with each succeeding generation.

The advent of the television solidified the worth of these gospel favorites. Stars from television shows like Andy Griffith and The Lawrence Welk Show began to sing these hymns on their shows and made albums. The music industry didn't fail to capitalize either. They brought forward stars like Tennessee Ernie Ford to produce albums with traditionally favored hymns.[16] Even Johnny Cash had

---

[16] York, Terry. 2003. Worship Wars. Hendrickson Publishing. Pages 41-48

his gospel albums.

The problem for the church is that the music industry didn't stop there. When musicians like Elvis began to sing these hymns they began to create new folk sounds that would become popular with those whom the singers were selling records to. This created a whole new era in Christian music. Soon Christian groups were not singing just Christian songs. Christian groups were being formed to sing a new genre of songs. It wasn't long before these songs began to find their way into church settings.

Soloists are allowed a sort of freedom to bring a message through song. The danger as perceived by the church was to allow the younger generation a musical voice. These young people began singing music that was unfamiliar to those who have always listened to the traditional favorites. (It is important to note that many songs contained in a hymnal are never sung. They are unfamiliar and people do not like to move very far from their comfort zone.) The music industry moved from soloist to groups with many instruments to entertain audiences. Churches were being asked if they could accommodate these same kinds of instruments in the church setting.

These changes fueled the "music wars". The older congregants began to feel that they were not being respected since their traditions were being pushed aside. They also felt strongly that music in church should be a corporate experience instead of an entertaining experience.

The younger generations felt that they were being disrespected because they could not listen to the style of music that made an emotional / spiritual impact on them.

So, here we have the two sides squaring off with each other: the older congregants standing firm in their tradition, and the youth deciding that they could play in another sandbox and leave the church altogether. They didn't have the long-standing tradition of commitment. They drifted to places that would meet their needs.

The difficult task for the KonXions music team is to find the right balance of music for each setting. The small group setting provides an arena that can draw like-minded individuals to gather together. These small groups can choose music that will fit their musical styles. The Regional Celebration Events select music that draws from the current popular cultural studies. Those attending these events will have opportunity to give feedback to the coordinators during and after the event. The leadership team will then study the requests to adjust the music to fit future events.

KonXions understands that God created all things under the sun. The music team is not required to play only Christian based music. Music must aid the congregant worship experience. "We try to create bridges that span the secular/sacred divide because we don't make that distinction. We use secular music in worship as well as film and literature. I hope they are points of connection between people's everyday lives and their faith."[17]

On music – Webber, after attending a charismatic church – left the church feeling tired from a steady diet of choruses without a change of pace. First he thought there was little substance to the songs. He felt that the idea was to keep the participant in a constant emotional state of enthusiasm. "I just wanted the noise to stop." Second, the music dominated over the text. Third, the music clashed with the text. The music must serve the venue of the service. It must all begin to find ways to work together.[18]

We have all attended church where the music left us flat. The KonXions music team's mission is to work with the leadership team, the multi-media team, and with members of the congregation to develop a song list that will enhance the overall worship experience. The worship team must develop a working schedule well in advance to allow enough time to develop each venue.

It is critical that all who are in attendance are in a full participation mode. It makes a difference when all are fully engaged. "Churches that want to experience God's transforming power in their worship must not overlook the importance of each individual's wholehearted participation. Worship is never something done to us for us, but always by us. Therefore, the church that desires worship renewal

---

[17]Gibbs, Eddie & Ryan K. Bolger. 2005. Emerging Churches. Baker Academic. Grand Rapids. Pages 67 & 68
[18]Webber, Robert E. 1996. Blended Worship. Hendrickson Publishers. Pages 108 - 110

must pay careful attention to its worship, giving people permission to participate and providing them adequate ways of truly becoming involved in worship."[19]

It is imperative to use the highest quality of music. "If the music sounds like junk, guests will assume the church is junk. If the service is sloppy and unplanned, they will assume the congregation does not have its act together. People demand and expect high quality music. God is a God of excellence. Our praise to God should be the best it can be."[20] KonXions seeks to master the issues around the music, visual arts and the liturgical aspects of each Event, either in the small group setting or at the Regional Celebration Events. We desire to present the best that we are able with each and every venue so that we can present our living God in the best light possible.

Historical Perspective on Technology within Ministry

Media, or what may be considered as being multimedia, within the church may seem to be a very new phenomenon for many traditional church members. Media ministry has been used though fairly consistently for the last several hundred years. Each generation has been

---

[19]Webber, Robert E. 1996. Blended Worship. Hendrickson Publishers.
    Page 84
[20]Ibid. Page 70

challenged by the entrance of some new form of technology. When Jesus taught the multitudes he incorporated a media technique that is still used today.

Examine the familiar story found in Luke 5:1-3. Jesus was standing next to Lake Gennesaret. The crowd began to press in so they could hear his every word. They were hungry to hear what Jesus had to say about the true God of Israel. Jesus noticed two fishing boats tied up nearby and the fishermen were cleaning the nets that were used during their night's fishing trip. He told Simon to pull his boat closer so he could climb aboard. Jesus then had Simon put the boat just a little way out into the waters. He settled himself comfortably on the floor of the boat and continued to minister to the crowd that had been pressing into him.

What was the technology that Jesus employed in this situation? First, you have to see clearly the physical environment in which Jesus was teaching. The shoreline was on the windward side of the lake. This means that the wind was coming off the lake and blowing toward the land. Jesus used the power of the wind to blow the sound of his voice into the crowd. The land near the lake rose up from the shoreline. The effect acted like an amphitheater. The sound of his voice would have been amplified as it was carried up the hill.

Jesus would have been aware of this concept from the Roman plays that were performed in the amphitheater found in Zeporous.   This theater could hold over four thousand people and the acoustics were perfect.   Actors whispering on the stage could be heard in all corners.

Between the time of Jesus and the Middle Ages media took the form of art. Worship for those attending mass was their opportunity to receive communion.   The message, which was in Latin, had little importance to those attending. Scripture was revealed to the masses through the use of pictorial story telling.   Paintings and stained glass windows were used to tell the stories of faith.

The world had lost the emphasis on writing skills during the medieval period.   Neither was the Holy Church interested in having the populace well educated.   Leaders of the church felt that scripture was not for the common person to read for themselves, but was to be translated for them by tradition through the priest and monks.

Jan Hus desired to bring reformation to the Catholic Church. His message was similar to that of Martin Luther. Hus was unable to get the message out to the multitudes that he and Luther felt were being held hostage by the church. How is it that Martin Luther was able to create a reformation that is still impacting the organized church today?   Hus was burned at the stake on July 6, 1415. He died just short of a major technological breakthrough that Luther had access to.   In 1444 the Gutenberg Press was invented.

Martin Luther was an astute priest who was willing to use all the resources that he had available to him. His decision to use the press was highly controversial. The Catholic Church felt very strongly that it was a mistake to put the Bible into the hands of common people, people who they felt did not have the proper training to understand the wisdom found in the depths of the mysteries hidden within the Bible. Luther went even further in his use of this new technology by having study materials available. He also used the press's ability to send out information quickly about various events, including his ninety-five theses that he nailed to the Castle Church door in Wittenberg. Due to Luther's ability to think that all culturally relevant tools were permissible, the Christian Church has flourished.

Today, walk into any church office and you will find laptops that create various documents used within the church. These computers have emptied the filing cabinets of unwanted paper reports. Copiers are connected wirelessly to all the computers in the church facility. Most of these copiers perform multiple tasks. They are used to send and receive faxes, scan documents for storage and they also replace the one-hour photo store. Cell phones keep the pastor connected to those who are privileged enough to know his number. Last, but not least, the Internet has become a staple that few could live without.

Flannel graphs are slowly being replaced with various styles of multi-media. The sanctuary of many older traditional churches has become the last vestige of the presumed holy. Many feel that any changes to the methods of worship are wrong. They become upset when the furnishings are moved or removed. They complain or leave because the music has become culturally relevant. They speak out when words on a screen replace their hymnal. Few feel comfortable when video clips are used to support the minister's sermon.

It is within this new media environment that KonXions seeks to become truly relevant with those in the target audience. Each and every day they are being bombarded with media on billboards, ads on their laptops as they search the Internet, television shows and sporting events that have built in commercial time for chips, cars, soft drinks, et cetera. KonXions seeks to study the current culture to stay relevant with each of the occurring shifts.

KonXion's Media Productions Missional Charge

This is the environment in which we minister to our Christian Community. Our challenge is to follow Captain Kirk with his missional statement: "To boldly go where no man [person] has gone before." We can boldly follow the footsteps of our forefathers in seeking new and challenging ways to present the Gospel to those who have been marginalized. We must break down the barriers that keep people from the Cross of Jesus.

Saint Francis of Assisi's wisdom has been followed by great leaders across time and space when he gave this advice: "Preach the gospel always. Use words when necessary." Each assignment given to Media Productions is another opportunity to weave words, music, art, still and moving images into ministerial pieces.

Media Productions partners with the leadership team to develop media that conveys the heart of the message. The culture that KonXions serves has become media saturated and accustomed to receiving information in more than one format. Messages must become more than just a set of words strung together to create meaningful points, but rather combined with other visual and audio mediums to create a more complete and fully understandable message.

The speaker's message has a stronger impact on the audience when the worship team creates a collaborative environment where all of the worship and media team members have the ability to shape the final message. The speaker sets the tone and the direction as led by the Holy Spirit. The senior staff leader in this collaborative effort becomes the chief visionary or prophet. Members of the team have freedom to make selections where there may be gaps in the message or provide alternative vehicles to deliver the message.

Media Productions when properly partnered with the leadership team creates Spirit-led ministry moments that impact lives for the Kingdom. Each assignment finds its focus based on the KonXions' mission and vision statements. These statements help direct both Media Productions plus the ministerial teams. It is important that those who participate in KonXions are able to clearly identify and define the KonXions Mission and Vision Statements: KonXions reason for being.

Mission Statement

"KonXions is breaking down barriers to the Cross of Jesus, by being culturally relevant."

Vision Statement

>KonXions seeks to minister to those who are between the ages of eighteen and thirty-five.

>KonXions seeks to use all forms of multi-media to: form connections; create a format where information is available for the KonXions community; to illustrate and heighten the message; and to inform the community of upcoming events.

>KonXions seeks to create environments where people can be themselves without the masks traditionally worn in spiritualized situations.

>KonXions seeks to allow people room to grow while they begin the process of seeking their missional opportunities.

KonXions

Implementation
Plan

KonXions Mission

Empowering the Local Church

KonXions visionary statement is this: "To reach those who have been marginalized within the mainline traditional church and those who may have never experienced Christ in the church setting." KonXions understands that its mission is not to eliminate the traditional church, but to allow the church to become relevant to a new generation. KonXions seeks to come along side of the traditional church to **Empower the Local Churches** for the mission that they has been given.

The church has the resources that KonXions can tap into for the success of its mission. Churches have a population that is perfect to reach those who are marginalized. This may sound strange knowing that this population is not effectively reaching those in the target audience, but KonXions feels that this older population has not been taught how to effectively engage the youth in meaningful ways. It is this older population that has children and grandchildren that they dearly love and seek to care for.

The church has successfully developed an army of pastors that have been educated either through seminary or a denominational course of study. These pastors are perfect to mentor the lay leaders who will be leading the small KonXional Groups.

The church has built within its structure individuals that are first committed to spreading the Good News: that we have hope for salvation through the one who died for our sins and who provided a method to become an heir to the King of Kings. These individuals are gifted by the Holy Spirit with musical talents, video and visual talents, leadership talents, supporting talents--the list continues. Where there is a need the Creative God provides.

Empower Laity and Clergy

Again, KonXions vision statement is: "To reach those who have been marginalized with the mainline traditional church and those who may have never experienced Christ in the church setting." It is only through the development of leadership will this mission ever be accomplished. Many mainline churches have a stringent program for their clergy members.

The Wesleyan Church does not require a pastor to complete seminary, but they do have a program of selected courses that can be completed at seminary, college, or through a course of study that is taught at the college level. The United Methodist Church has two tracks for their clergy. The first track leads the clergy to an Elder position. The clergy member must complete seminary to reach Elder. The second track is only slightly less stringent. The church has developed a course of study that is produced by the seminaries. The clergy member going through this process obtains a Local Preacher License.

KonXions will **Empower this ready-made Supply of Clergy**. KonXions seeks to find those pastors that have a natural connection with the target audience. These pastors will be recruited to act as mentors for the laity-- KonXional Interpreters--as they take leadership positions. These pastors may find themselves involved as special speakers at Regional Celebration Events or also used as seminar leaders.

The early Methodist Church relied on Circuit Riders to reach all of the little communities that could not afford to have their own pastor each week. Their mission was to provide these small groups with the Sacrament on a quarterly basis. They also mentored the local Interpreters in all areas of ministry. KonXions allows clergy to continue in their current charge or station as they work with the Interpreters in their area. This provides oversight and consistency for the small KonXional Groups.

Empower the KonXional Groups into Ministry

As they say: "This is where the rubber hits the road." The Regional Celebration Events has two missions. The first is to provide an atmosphere where the participants find a comfortable and safe environment in which they are allowed to express themselves as they worship the Triune God. The second purpose of the Event is to provide an avenue for those attending to find a home within a small KonXional Group.

Each small KonXional group is encouraged to bring others to Events and to meetings. These two outlets should provide an atmosphere where they would desire to bring others to share the experience. It is also part of the DNA of KonXions to provide or to encourage the small KonXional Groups outreach missions. These missional opportunities may be as diverse as the groups who are lead by the Spirit to imagine them

It is in these small groups that deep, long lasting relationships can be built. When these individuals come together under their Interpreter's direction they are guided into a deeper relationship with the Triune God. It is here that each person will find that God loved them so much that a savior was provided. Each one of us also has the power of the Holy Spirit dwelling in us so that they can then begin to follow the model of Jesus.

Action Step One (Engaging the Local Church)

1-The KonXional Media department shall create a multi-layer approach for the promotion of KonXional Ministry within the local congregations. The Media team will utilize: Website presence, bulletin inserts, email news-release, posters and banners, road side statement signage and media news releases for radio, print and television.

2-Members of the KonXional Team will be available for personal presentations to local churches. These presentations may include worship, small group settings, women and men meetings, and Administration Council Meetings.

3-KonXions will develop and implement local workshops for engaging the local church to reach outside of their walls, develop laity leadership, design and implement strategies for reaching both family and friends. The Communications team will develop: training manuals, power point presentations and promotional flyers.

4-KonXional Leaders will help organize and run the KonXional groups until the Interpreters are fully operational. Circuit Riders will then be in place for continual mentoring and monitoring. KonXions will work with previously established small groups in local churches to further equip them.

Action Step Two (Multi-media formation)

1-KonXions will purchase computer programming to allow for video conferencing between individuals and churches. Skype will work for small meetings where one or two are missing. There are programs that have the ability to connect large numbers of people. This will save time and money for individual travel.

2-KonXions worship team works to either purchase or develop curriculum that will target the needs of the KonXional Group and KonXional Event. This curriculum will mainly be video based and accessible through the KonXions Website or through the mail.

3-KonXions' Facebook is for individuals to find resource materials, make virtual connections, and to find out the latest news and scheduled events.

4-KonXions will maintain a presence on Facebook and other media outlets.

Action Step Three (Curriculum Purchase)

1-KonXions will develop a library of video based curriculum to meet the needs of the individual groups.

KonXions has the ability to draw first from the United Methodist Conference libraries, churches involved in the KonXions, and finally, purchase additional materials from outside sources.

2-KonXions will put this information onto the KonXional website as copyright laws allow. KonXions will continue to work with the various producers to allow this. There may be an additional charge for usage. The purpose of this is to maintain the original integrity of the product and also to save on shipping and handling costs.

Action Step Four (Regional Events with Seminars)

1-Regional Training Events are scheduled as needed to encourage the local church ministry team.

Action Step Five (Regional Events include children and Youth Activities)

1-KonXions understands that some in the target audience have children that could (or should) participate. KonXions seeks to meet the needs of these families by developing a team of individuals that have a passion for children and youth.

2-KonXions goal at the time of this writing is to fully stock a trailer with sound and light equipment, supplies to play wide area games and stunts, equipment to set up a safe play area, and equipment necessary to develop a child care area for those parents that need to have their child cared for while attending an Event.

Leadership and Spiritual

Action Step One (Laity Development)

1-Recruiting Interpreters (internal) – Interpreters and Circuit Riders will work together in indentifying those who are called to start their own KonXional Group.

2-Recruiting Interpreters (external) – The KonXional Leadership Team (consisting of Circuit Riders) will be intentionally looking for individuals that have a love for God and desire to serve God in meaningful ways. It is critical that KonXions works with local college pastors and others on campuses to identify potential Interpreters.

3-KonXional Media Department is dedicated to supply promotional literature for the purpose of recruiting.

4-KonXional Media Department will work with local secular and Christian radio stations to supply ads for the purpose of recruiting Interpreters.

5-KonXional Media Department and the KonXional Leadership Team will create a booth that can be set up at major KonXional Events and/or other events that would attract our targeted audience.

6-Training sessions will be held regularly to involve individuals quickly.

Actions Step Two (Clergy Development)

1-The leadership team is continually on the watch to identify those clergy who have completed the Course of Study or have completed seminary. These clergy must have a proven track record in ministering to those in the targeted audience.

2-The leadership team will support the clergy as they begin to participate as Circuit Riders. Each clergy would be responsible for either an area or a number of Interpreters.

3-The leadership team will continue to develop new programs that will educate the clergy on how the Interpreters will run a KonXional Group as well as to how to maintain a healthy KonXional Group.

4-Encourage each Circuit Rider to be personally involved in KonXional Group for their own well being.

Action Step Three (Monthly Check-in Meetings)

1-The KonXional Leadership Team will meet monthly with the Circuit Riders.

2-The Circuit Riders will hold monthly Interpreter meeting for additional training.

Reaching our Neighbors – Building relationship with our neighbors, particularly with those who have been disenfranchised by mainstream society.

Action Step One (Attraction of our Global Neighbors)

The goal of this particular Action Step is to go to sporting events, parks, parking lots and holiday events to reach out into the community with a team of people who are willing to be the presence of Christ.

1-At the time of this writing the leadership team has envisioned a traveling entertainment trailer. This trailer will be equipped with sound equipment and designed to set up in parking lots or in parks. The trailer itself will turn into a sound stage.

2-Develop a traveling barbeque pit that will be able to serve up to five hundred or more hamburgers and hot dogs.

3-Develop a promotional DVD that can be handed out to those who come by for the music or for the food.

4-Develop a worship team that can play both secular and spiritual music that will draw crowds to the ministry area.

5-Develop a team of individuals that can interact with guests to the traveling Event. The mission is to find those who would like to become involved in KonXional

Groups and a second goal would be to identify future Interpreters.

Action Step Two (Missional Opportunities)

1-KonXional leadership team will continue to work providing local, regional and global opportunities for groups that cannot find activities on their own.

2-Develop connections with volunteer coordinators to find projects that each group could participate in.

Action Step Three (Regional Events)

1-The leadership team will continuously seek out new opportunities for Regional Events.

Event Ideas:

Hog Wild – Motorcycle trek with a pig roast at the end of the trail. Tattoo artist could be on hand for consultations and performance.

Concert in the Park – Movie Night at a Drive-in – Game night at a sporting event tagging onto other's Events (Family Life Network concerts) – Water Events – Camping

KonXions

KonXional Group

Training Manual

KonXions

Index of Contents

Dear Participant,

I have longed for an opportunity to develop my passion for reaching those who are very similar to me. I have loved to hate the organized church. I find it very interesting that God has chosen me to be a representative of God's Kingdom. When I look around I see so many more that are highly qualified. Here in lies the rub, they are doing nothing with the talents God has given to them. I guess Paul was right when he said that God will use the lowly to confuse the wise.

The first part of the book was mainly theory to prove to those who may doubt the need for a new blue print for doing "church." Now in the following pages Craig and I will try to give you hands on training on how small KonXional Groups should or could look like.

I want to thank a mentor of mine. Much of the following pages are similar to his seminar. Rev. Dan Finch is truly a prophetic voice calling all clergy and laity to get involved.

Now is the time, Join the Revolutions,

Stephen Crowell, Senior Pastor of KonXions

Orientation / Check-in

This first section is for the KonXional Leadership who is planning and running Circuit Rider and Interpreter leadership training seminars. Just as this is a training manual for Circuit riders and Interpreters the Leadership Team must also be briefed and reminded how to operate.

Welcome Center Signage

Excellence can never be replaced. Each meeting is a representation of God's love for each and every one of us. It is critical to get it right. Just this last week I went to a rather large important meeting for pastors in our area, I was surprised that the street had zero signage to let me know that I had arrived. The church didn't have anyone posted to welcome me or to let me know where the restroom was (it was quite a long drive). Upon entering I had to find my way to the room where we were to meet. I was not impressed. As we continue to grow and develop let us continue to pay attention to the details.

It is critical that proper informational signage is placed outside in appropriate locations, such as the roadside, so that anyone coming to the event will have clear and precise directions. The signs that are produced must be professional in nature with plenty of white space.

Event staff must be in place early and set-up well in advance of the first guest. Guests tend to arrive early because they are unsure of where they should go after arriving on site.

Ensure that all areas of the event are clean and ready for guests. Make a through sweep of the place to ensure that restrooms are in full working order. Also make sure that they are easily assessable and properly marked.

Each and every person regardless of pride will wear event lanyards with name and position. This will ensure that all are placed at ease from the start. It makes one, especially me, uncomfortable when you may know someone and cannot remember their name. (Take it from me I find myself in this predicament often.)

Music must be playing and upbeat. Silence is the death of Americans. We do not do well without it. Make proper arrangements.

Have the equipment set-up well in advance to ensure that all issues have been worked out. Keep plenty of spares and replacements. Prepare for the worst possible situation.

Have the sign-in table clear of junk and be ready with material well in advance. Make it look as inviting as possible.

These small items set the pace for the "event"!!!

The Check-in

The Check-in is a series of questions that acts as a vehicle to help the KonXional Group become closer to each other and to help avoid any issues during a meeting. These questions should be asked early on in each of your meetings. This time gives each person a chance to unload anything that maybe weighing them down. Remember the group is about relationships.

Also, along this line please be extremely careful to not let this become a place for unhealthy conversation or a place for one individual to use as a place to repeatedly receive positive affirmation. Honestly, this is a tricky area to wade through. The more the group meets together the more the group will help to control this section of the meeting.

John Wesley had this incorporated in his Class and Band Meetings. He had four questions that were asked each time. These were related to their spiritual practice, like do you have any known sin in your life. In our meetings the emphasis may be along similar lines, but with a little more tact. It should also be noted that a person can pass on the question.

Questions that could be asked:

What is the best or worse that has happened to you since we last met?

What is it that holds your mental attention lately?

Is there a white elephant or the eight hundred pound gorilla in the room that we should talk about?

Is there anything that one just has to share for the good of the body?

Make up your own questions.

Again, the goal is to help build the process of intimacy and to clear the air before the lesson begins.

The Welcome

It is critical to keep the energy level high and to engage everyone in conversations. This may be the first time that these individuals are getting together so it is important to help them feel comfortable.

It is *critical* that the event starts on time and ends on time. No exceptions.

The Welcome

Have the host for the area welcome the guests to the event. It is important to give out the entire house keeping information right in the beginning. This also puts people to rest.

Begin with self-introduction: include name, position, and what you expect to get out of the event. Also, devolve something unique that would be interesting about you, the more unique and amusing the notation the better.

As much as we may all hate it, it is important to go around the room and make sure we introduce ourselves to everyone.

Next, start with an Ice-Breaker Activity that should last about five minutes.

Introduce the first Speaker. Be upbeat, positive and concentrate on their achievements.

Session One

KonXions Introduction Series

A} Why I longed for a connectional group!

Stephen's Personal Story

I am sure that many of you may not even be sure why you're here participating in a KonXional Training Seminar. Yet, I know that it is not by chance. You see I believe in a God that sets out to call the created back into a relationship with the Creator. Like lead character Gibbs on NCIS, I don't believe in coincidence. You were destined to be here; what you do with your experience is entirely up to you. I don't know what brought you here, but I think it is important for you to know why I began to develop KonXions. Over the next few pages I will share with you my faith journey and where I found my true foundation.

If I could I would take you to one of my favorite places on this earth. Picture this: a cabin deep in the woods with a stream running down in the ravine. This was my retreat during my childhood years. I would walk in these woods and it was there that I felt at peace. Over time I have brought my special friends here to experience it with me; today I invite you walk with me in these woods as I explain why KonXions was birthed.

It is extremely important for children in their developmental stage to find and understand their identity within the boundaries of: who they are; who created them; and with whom they share their space. I thought I knew who I was until my classmates began talking about being German, English, French or whatever. I began to realize that I had no true known background. I struggled during my youth to understand the world in which I lived.

I thought it had to do with being adopted. There became a hole in my life that I could not fill. No matter what I did, I knew that a piece was missing. I began to challenge my parents with asking questions about my past. They were not able to give me very many answers, because then the adoption information was sealed. I didn't have to worry about my place in the family since I had always been secure in my relationship with my parents. Yet, the outside world continued to ask questions that I was not prepared to understand.

My life became very tumultuous.

Life became gray where I thought it should be black and white. I grew up in church where Christian principles were outlined. Outside of church though I rarely saw these principles lived out in people that I worshiped with other than my parents. My parents set standards and followed them. Yet, I played in other people's homes and their lifestyles didn't add up to what I saw them to pretend to be on Sunday.

I kept looking for ways to fill that void in my soul. I tried drugs to kill the pain. I used unhealthy relationships to fill the void. I tried to live life on the edge where it didn't matter if I lived or died. I even tried to live a very good life and never seemed to live up to expectations.

Finally, I told God that if he wanted me then he would have to come after me, I was done with his kind of religion. I wanted to get away from the trappings that held me down. I wanted to fill that persistent hole in my soul. I left home the summer of my high school graduation.

God took me up on my challenge. It didn't matter that I ran as far away from my home and roots as I could. God sought me out and changed my world.

My life turned around between the darkness of one evening and the early morning of the next day. In Texas I met God in a very unusual way. I literally drowned while in a drug induced state. Yet somehow I found myself on a dock far from where I had started out on the shore the evening before. As I began to wake up to the pain of fire ants biting my legs I knew that God had saved me both physically and spiritually. I was ready to go where God called me.

I returned home to begin a Youth Ministry at my father's church. We were allowed to become very unique in our approach in our style of ministry. We were very creative in how the Good News was presented. We built our group around five basic elements that have been around since the "body of believers" was recorded in the book of Acts.

Still though I was not thrilled with what I saw in the Mainline Traditional Church setting. I could see then that the "church" was not able to reach many of the outsiders. I thought like the rest that a change had to be made. What became popular at the time were the church growth movements. I jumped into this line of thought to the point where I started a master's program in "Church Growth." I thought at the time that my ideas on how church should be operated were strange.

Through a series of God ordained events I found my home as a camp director. It was here that I introduced people of all ages to God in very natural settings. We hosted groups on the weekends that were small and intimate. It was in this type of setting that they could become themselves. The boundaries of the church were gone. They ate together and took time out to get to know each other. Strange things began to happen, like they actually could hear the voice of God more clearly and had the opportunity to interact more with what they were learning.

After losing my job as the camp director, I found myself back in the church. I also lost my first wife during this time. I didn't find the answers I needed in church. I would go each Sunday out of a sense of duty. I sat on the hard bench. There was a man who sat in front of me each week. He didn't know my name and I didn't know his. We shook hands and smiled as if it was all okay. I knew in my heart of hearts that all I would do is sit and watch his hair get grayer and thinner. Where was the love of God that was promised me? I wanted to throw my mask off and say who I truly was. I was in a room full of people who said they cared, but I felt completely alone.

I was asked if I would join a small group of men to study God's word and to build relationships. Finally, I found what I had been looking for. I had been saved most of my life. I had Jesus come into my heart and become Lord of my life. But, I was doing it on my own. Now, I had others to be the hands and feet that Jesus offered in the Word. I had a place where the mask came off. I had Freedom to be who I was without pretending. I had a place where I could experience Hope. I also saw that I had Freedom from those dark feelings that kept me awake at night. I learned what true stewardship was. I began to see the truth of what I had been preaching and teaching about for so long. I knew that I was home and that this was the model that I wanted to start to help others find their own Hope.

Most of all I wanted to find ways to break down all the barriers that keep people from the Cross of Jesus. Jesus is kept from those inside and out of the churches because of traditions.

"Check In" Questions:

If able and you feel safe, please give us brief account of your story and why you decided to be here.

B} KonXions Overview

Let me lay a foundation for what our expectations are for KonXional groups. KonXions is all about building relationships with the Triune God and with others who will walk with you in the good times and through the rough times. Jesus modeled various ways in which to live our lives. KonXions, as a body of believers, desires to follow these models that Jesus set for us.

One life style Jesus modeled was that He would enjoy a meal with anyone that would sit with him. Jesus is seen eating his way through the Gospels. Another way in which Jesus modeled for KonXions was he developed deep-rooted relationships. Those of us in KonXions desire to build deep relationships with each other and in that process with the Triune God. These relationships are built within each area of our being together, but specifically through spending quantity of time together. One word for this would be **Fellowship.**

It is my idea that you are here searching for truth. Our mission is to open the living Word of God and reveal truths that are hidden in what was thought to be a dry boring book that condemned people to Hell. The Bible is instead filled with unending true principles given to us by the creator so that we could live extremely productive and enjoyable lives. KonXions is a safe place to allow transformation to begin. Another model Jesus gave to us was time spent learning about the things of God and the Kingdom of God. The twelve were called disciples because they were learners. We also follow in this process so we too are becoming **Disciples**.

In Jeremiah we find that the Lord God created humanity with a plan to do great things.

Jeremiah 29:11-13 (NRSV) For surely I know the plans I have for you, says the LORD, plans for your welfare and not for harm, to give you a future with hope. Then when you call upon me and come and pray to me, I will hear you. When you search for me, you will find me; if you seek me with all your heart,

We also find in Ephesians 2:10 (NRSV) that we are God's Workmanship. *For we are what he has made us, created in Christ Jesus for good works, which God prepared beforehand to be our way of life.* God prepared for us in advance a plan to do good works so that God would receive the glory.

God has given each of us special talents. Each one of us has been called to do extremely wonderful things for others. The entire twelfth chapter of I Corinthians reveals to us that each one is given one or more gifts for the common good of all. KonXions is modeled after the second part of the chapter where one body is served by its many parts.

KonXions is committed to developing each individual and group's talents to serve others. Our mission is to find ways to help each other and also those who are outside of the group. Healthy groups find one or more ways to become **Outward Focused.**

The leadership of KonXions is committed to find unique **Worship** experiences. Each region is charged to develop regular events where the different KonXional groups will join to corporately worship together in meals, concerts, and teaching moments. Worship is not contained to one style of activities or to specific locations. Worship will also be incorporated into the weekly lesson plans.

Lastly, KonXions is concerned about the souls of humanity. Since Adam and Eve turned their backs on their creator the soul of each person has become clouded. Each person needs to respond to the calling of the Holy Spirit with repentance through faith and then allow Jesus to be Lord of their life. It is then that an individual can begin to turn their life towards the Light of the World. When people die to self they begin to have new life. Each KonXional groups will have opportunity to reach those in their sphere of influence to bring the Good News of Salvation to outsiders with acts of **Ministry.**

KonXions seeks to reach out to those who are currently resistant to attend a traditional mainline church, or any church for that matter. Many have become extremely cynical of the church. Not because they haven't tried attending, it is because they have attended and did not like what they saw. David Kinnaman in his book "Un

Christian" claims through research that there are twenty-four million outsiders in this country who are ages sixteen to twenty-nine.[21] KonXions believes that we have a Ministry to reach these individuals with the gospel message in a package that they will relate too. It is time to use all the technology at our disposal combined with true relational opportunities. No longer will we use tried formulas to reach these outsiders--other than truly seeking to build a bridge of friendship with them.

Jesus traveled for three years with twelve men who became known as the Disciples. Many others traveled with Jesus as well to learn more about the Kingdom of God. According to the plan that was before the foundations of the Earth were even laid, Jesus set his sights on Jerusalem for his final hours. Jesus used the backdrop of Passover to free the people one more time. It was during this last week that Jesus took extra care to share the truths of Kingdom with the Disciples.

We have all experienced either through movies, television or even through real life that a person who is about to pass away speaks only those words that have deep meaning to them. Jesus was no different. He used every opportunity offered to give more and more truth. It was in this mode that Jesus used the trickery of the Sadducees and the Pharisees to teach about what was truly important to him and to his Father. In Mathew twenty-two the Pharisees

---

[21] Kinnaman, David. 2007. Un Christian. Baker Books. Page18

come to Jesus to trick him so they could have him arrested. They needed to have Jesus removed from society to prevent any more from leaving their faith.

Matthew 22:34-40 (NRSV) When the Pharisees heard that he had silenced the Sadducees, they gathered together, and one of them, a lawyer, asked him a question to test him. "Teacher, which commandment in the law is the greatest?" He said to him, "'You shall love the Lord your God with all your heart, and with all your soul, and with all your mind.' This is the greatest and first commandment. And a second is like it: 'You shall love your neighbor as yourself.' On these two commandments hang all the law and the prophets."

The story continues after Jesus rose from the grave. He met with his Disciples again before leaving for heaven. Jesus gave the one more command on which they should base their ministry. This command is found in Mathew twenty-eight.

Matthew 28:18-20 (NRSV) And Jesus came and said to them, "All authority in heaven and on earth has been given to me. Go therefore and make disciples of all nations, baptizing them in the name of the Father and of the Son and of the Holy Spirit, and teaching them to obey everything that I have commanded you. And remember, I am with you always, to the end of the age."

The first set of verses we consider to be <u>The Greatest Commandments</u> and the second as <u>The Great Commission.</u> The early mothers and fathers of the church understood these to be foundation on which to build. These truths are what Jesus claims to be the most important. KonXions desires to return to these foundational truths.

We first believe that our mission is to be relational. In our relationships we begin to learn to love the Triune God more and more. As we begin to love the Father, the Son and the Holy Spirit more and more we begin to have the power from the Spirit to love others more. We even have the ability to find ways to love ourselves. KonXions believes that as we begin to love the Triune God more our life will begin to become transformed by the working of the Holy Spirit. We have no ability to change anyone, nor should we try.

1John 1:1-7 (NRSV) We declare to you what was from the beginning, what we have heard, what we have seen with our eyes, what we have looked at and touched with our hands, concerning the word of life-- this life was revealed, and we have seen it and testify to it, and declare to you the eternal life that was with the Father and was revealed to us-- we declare to you what we have seen and heard so that you also may have fellowship with us; and truly our fellowship is with the Father and with his Son Jesus Christ. We are writing these things so that our joy may be complete. This is the message we have heard from him and proclaim to you, that God is light and in him there is no darkness at all. If we say that we have fellowship with him while we are walking in darkness, we lie and do not do what is true; but if we walk in the light as he himself is in the light, we have fellowship with one another, and the blood of Jesus his Son cleanses us from all sin.

KonXions is comprised of small KonXional groups connected with each other through the website www.konXions.org where people can connect with each other, down load weekly lessons and also videos that contain teaching moments. Each KonXional group will be connected with a leader--a Circuit Rider--who will guide and support as needed. Regional events will provide both fellowship and training events that will also contain elements of corporate worship. KonXions is sanctioned through the United Methodist Church. The Senior Visionary Pastor is Stephen Crowell who is currently shepherding four local churches in Western New York. Craig Buelow is the Associate Pastor who is helping to develop KonXional Groups as well.

Check-in Questions

What are the five Foundational Building Blocks of the early church and KonXions?

1} _____

2} _____

3} _____

4} _____

5} _____

Who are being marginalized from the church?

What do you think about the number of those who are in our targeted range of Outsiders? What challenges do we face with this group of people?

What are the two Foundational Scriptures that both the early church and KonXions use and what are they called?

1} _____ - _____

2} _____ - _____

What are the primary goals for each KonXional group?

We are to build _____.

With whom? _____

Who is responsible for changing the lives of those we minister too?

What is our role in helping others?

Your thoughts so far?

C} Outdated Ideas

Please turn to the previous section of this book with the title "Outdated Ideas" – starting on page 21. After rereading this section please answer the following questions.

Check-in Questions

What has been your experience with the mainline traditional church?

Do these statistics sound reasonable to you or do you think these have been skewed somehow?

What are some of the other barriers that church has raised that has kept so many people from attending?

What can KonXions do to change the way people think about following Christ?

What do you think is important to have included in our actions and activities?

Would you consider becoming a radical believer of Jesus and his teaching and be willing to look at the Bible in its original context instead of seeing it through North American lenses?

Is so, where do you think the problems are with how we have come to see things today? (One example is that churches tend to be filled with those that have things and Jesus said that he came to reach those that needed help.

Luke 4:18 & 19 (NRSV) "The Spirit of the Lord is upon me, because he has anointed me to bring good news to the poor. He has sent me to proclaim release to the captives and recovery of sight to the blind, to let the oppressed go free, to proclaim the year of the Lord's favor.")

Session Two

KonXional Interpreters

A} Hear Their Stories!

Janis

Janis is a single mom, who has attended church her entire life. In fact her father was a pastor for many years. Janis grew up in the church and has served the church faithfully in youth groups, Sunday School, worship, and in Vacation Bible School. She couldn't live with the pain anymore and pulled out completely.

"I can't go back anymore. I am tired of people; it takes too much energy to go." Why - "Because they are all hypocrites. They come to church and pretend to be something other than who they really are. But, it doesn't end there. I am the chief of the hypocrites. I pretend that I don't smoke and that I am sleeping with my boyfriend. I can't tell them who I really am, so I have pretended to be this person that I am not. I would not be accepted if they knew the truth about me. I am tired." Janis goes on to tell that she still loves God and wants to follow Jesus. But it hurts too much to be around those who have false expectations.

Lisa

Lisa is an older single woman, who lives alone in a very small apartment. She has taken care of many children over the years. She has worked hard to take care of herself. I wouldn't call it extreme pride but a great sense of identity. My wife, Kristan, was talking to her one day and the conversion turned to church. In part it was that she was embarrassed that I saw her smoking on her porch. She knew that I was a pastor and felt guilty for her behavior. Kristan quickly put her fears aside and said that it didn't matter to me. The rest of her words that I could hear while working on fixing some of her windows hurt my soul.

"I can't go to any of the churches in town. They are filled with hypocrites. I have lived here too long not to know the truth about them. They act so well on Sunday. Even my sister, who goes to church, tells me I am going to hell because of the stuff I do. I love God. I watch pastors on television. I read my Bible everyday and read my devotionals."

Kristan let her know that she was loved by God.

Carl

I met Carl once in a church setting that was for a special event for a family member. Our true conversion started in a hospital room where he was visiting a relative. The relative mentioned to me that I needed to convince him to return to church. Pain shot across his face before he answered her.

"Pastor, don't even try. I won't go back. It is not that I don't love God. I meet him in my own way. I pray all of the time and read the Bible. It is those people at church that I can't be around."

My own son, Stephen

Stephen grew up as a pastor's child. It was while I was a camp director that he slipped away from the church. We sent him to youth meetings where they had opportunity to smoke and drink. He hung out with church families that acted completely different during the week than on Sunday.

Stephen ended up going to private Christian school. Again he saw the character of people who called themselves Christian. People pretended in public to be other than who they were in private. This totally pissed him off.

As soon as he could he ran as far away as possible. He went to Thailand where he could explore alternative religions. He came back seeing a commitment to their beliefs not found here.

He knew though that ultimately Christ was needed for his salvation. But, he cannot get over the word "church." In fact, his conversations with his friends show that they all feel the same way. Just the word "church" sends them into the shivers. Church is a loaded word with too many bad memories.

Check-in Questions

Would you think that people in the "church" would agree with these statements?

Why or Why Not?

How would you overcome the idea of being hypocritical? Can any one of us follow the rules?

Is this even the point? What is the Good News?

B} Message to the Interpreters

I want you to know how proud I am of you to take this first step into the unknown. You have made a huge step in becoming an Interpreter with KonXions. This is where you can receive awesome training to help others begin to reconnect with the "body of Christ." It is within KonXional Groups or small groups that people can truly become part of the DNA. It takes all kinds of people from all different walks of life to create a whole.

I know that you can do this. You more than likely came with all kinds of questions and doubts that you are able and capable to become an Interpreter. You have heard this title before. Let me take the time to explain exactly what an Interpreter is within a KonXional Group. Interpreters help to lead group discussion after watching a video tape. The leadership team has prepared lesson plans for each session. Each week your regional leader will be available to help you with any questions that you may have concerning the lessons or anything else that may come up.

Some of you may think that you don't have the right education or you didn't go to seminary. It doesn't matter. In truth we prefer that you didn't go to seminary. If you did you would most likely end up talking like a pastor and speak over the heads of those are in front of you. We are led by the working of the Holy Spirit. Let me tell you, I know that you can do it. Why? Because if you are breathing and willing to lead God will use you. God doesn't call the Equipped, but equips the Called. God will give you the wisdom as you need it. Besides, it doesn't hurt to say: "You know that is a good question and I am not sure what the answer is, but I know where I can get the answer for you!"

The Bible lets us know that if we ask for wisdom God will surely provide the wisdom when needed. I am sure that you will be like Joshua when Moses laid hands on him to take over the leadership of the Hebrew Children. Joshua knew how difficult it had been over the last forty years in the wilderness. He must have been afraid that he wouldn't know how to lead them into the Promised Land. Yet, we read in Deuteronomy how he overcame his fear.

Deuteronomy 34:9 (NRSV) Now Joshua son of Nun was filled with the spirit of wisdom because Moses had laid his hands on him. So the Israelites listened to him and did what the LORD had commanded Moses.

The Spirit of Wisdom or the Holy Spirit filled Joshua with the wisdom that he needed as he needed it. I know that God will give you not only the wisdom, but the strength, the energy, and the ability to handle what may come. Like Paul who ministered to those living in Philippi, he didn't think that he had what it took to minister there. Thing didn't always go well, but with God he knew that he could do all things through Christ who gave him the strength (Philippians 4:13).

The Interpreters of the local KonXional Groups become the core to our leadership. This is where the main ministry happens. When you make the commitment to lead a group you become part of an elite band of Christ followers. You become the life-line to thousands and thousands of people that we cannot reach on our own. Just think of how a church is limited to its permanent location. With the flexibility of our small KonXional Groups we can go anywhere two or more are gathered.

Just as Jesus left the twelve standing looking at the sky with a commission on them to reach into the entire world, I now use the power and authority given by God to Commission you to begin your ministry. You have the power given to you by scripture to fulfill the Great Commission and the Great Commandments. Like Jesus modeled for us, you are to reach out with the Good News. The News is that they can be forgiven for their sins and have a right relationship with their God.

What I need to communicate with you is that your commitment to KonXions matters to the "Body of Christ." The "Body of Christ" cannot grow without our KonXional Groups growing. That is why I am so grateful to you that you are willing to make this step of faith. As you make your commitment to become a leader or an Interpreter our leadership staff makes a commitment to you. We will pray for you regularly and find ways to continually lift you up before our Lord.

We know that you act as the Army Rangers or the Navy Seal or the Marine Special Operations. You are an elite force that will offer a unique opportunity that other small groups may not offer. You will help lead your KonXional Group not only in Bible study, but with finding ways to fellowship, worship, reach out to others who are seeking a relationship with God, and to find creative ways to use your groups combined talents to reach into the community, region or even globally. It is our privilege to stand alongside of you.

The power of KonXional Groups is that we offer all of the five components. Each is great on their own, but the power of transformation is when all five are combined together. New life begins to grow when we work together to complete tasks, and intimacy comes when we learn to not only fellowship, but seek for God to show up in our lives.

I feel it is important to let you know now that your attendance at this training is not an accident. I believe that God, before the foundations of the physical earth were even laid, prepared you for this moment:

Ephesians 1:4-12 (NRSV) just as he chose us in Christ before the foundation of the world to be holy and blameless before him in love. He destined us for adoption as his children through Jesus Christ, according to the good pleasure of his will, to the praise of his glorious grace that he freely bestowed on us in the Beloved. In him we have redemption through his blood, the forgiveness of our trespasses, according to the riches of his grace that he lavished on us. With all wisdom and insight he has made known to us the mystery of his will, according to his good pleasure that he set forth in Christ, as a plan for the fullness of time, to gather up all things in him, things in heaven and things on earth. In Christ we have also obtained an inheritance, having been destined according to the purpose of him who accomplishes all things according to his counsel and will, so that we, who were the first to set our hope on Christ, might live for the praise of his glory.

After reading this passage one would have to believe that God has been preparing you for this moment in time. Each of your past experiences has prepared you for becoming the leader of the Group that God has called you to. You would never have guessed that when you went through those tough times that it would or could be used to give glory and honor to God.

What we ask of you at this time to be an Interpreter is to be a growing Christian and an authentic believer. The last thing we want is to have someone pretending or faking it. We are looking for people to be transparent. It is when we share from our weakness that we truly begin to grow. What I need for you to do is relax.

Many may feel that achieving the best lesson or developing the best event is what is necessary for success. What is truly necessary is that we are come together to form relationships. We will walk with you as you begin to develop your KonXional Group. We will pray with you and give you advice. Your regional leader will act as a coach and mentor. Like the Marines we intend to leave no one behind.

Check-in Questions

How are you able to host a KonXional Group without a Seminary Education?

What can you learn from the report of Moses, a leader, laying hands of Joshua, the next leader of the stiff necked Hebrew children? Deuteronomy 34:9

What makes KonXional Groups most productive?

What proof do you have that you are destined to be part of KonXions?

I want to take this time to pray with you a prayer of Commissioning.

It would be good to go around the room and to lay hands on each individual.

C} KonXional Group Simulation

It is important during this training to actually experience what a KonXional Group could look like. I want to emphasize "could" because each KonXional Group will not necessarily look like any other KonXional Group.

Groups grow organically like the cells in the body. A skin cell works well when it multiplies as a skin cell. Likewise KonXional Groups will draw groups of people that have several similar traits. These traits in many ways will become fashioned after you, the Interpreter. When you begin to develop your KonXional Group you will most likely draw from those who are in your Inner Circle. We will talk about that at a later time.

What is important for this exercise is to understand that all five of the Core Requirements (fellowship, discipleship, worship, mission, and evangelism) may not be used at each meeting or event. One example where this would be evident could be at a tail gate event; it may not be the place where you practice being missional or evangelistic. On the other hand if your group has taken on the mission of helping cash strapped families or individuals by fixing their cars, you would not bring tailgate party food.

We will discuss at a later time where KonXional Groups can take place. Today we will use a typical living room setting. Without getting lost, let's move to the KonXional Group area.

Note for Instructor: An area should be already setup for this activity. You will need to have a Laptop with projector or a TV with a DVD player. Chairs or Living Room Setting should be set up. This should also be in another room that is small so as to create the actual atmosphere.

The Gathering

(Sample, this may look a thousand different ways.)

During the gathering it is important to connect with each person as they are coming to ensure that they are comfortable and connected with others. Take time to offer them a drink or a something to put into their hands. People need something in their hands. After a short bit of time get everyone settled down for the meeting. You could use this time for some announcements.

Check-in

What is it that you have been thinking most about in the last two weeks?

(If the group is less than 15, have each one share. If more than, break up into smaller groups.)

Worship Moment

Have three candles placed on a table that has been made into an alter. Light the candles one at a time inviting the Creator, Savior, and Sustainer into the meeting.

Celebrate God's work in our life by Faithfully Giving to God what is Gods by giving an offering. (This can be done with passing a basket or having one available to put money during the break. This could be just a time of prayer for KonXions as a whole and the ministry that is being completed.)

Fellowship

Take time out to have a snack.

While snacking take time to participate in a finding out about those on the journey with you.

Discipleship

Pop in DVD and follow the Prepared Lesson Plan

The DVD may have a trailer that has a Stewardship Moment

Session Three

KonXional Group (Breaking it Down)

A} Before you begin

The KonXional Group starts long before you sit across from someone in your meeting place. This section is where we begin to twist the nuts onto the bolts and put it all together. Every KonXional Group needs to have a starting place. It begins with you the Interpreter Leader. You will need to have a clear and precise concept of where you are going to go with you group. You become the captain of you own ship. The captain determines the destination and the best plan to get the ship to its final port. The captain is also in charge of all the phases of the operations. A great captain also knows how to check in with their headquarters often and as needed.

It is important to again make the strong statement;

"Connecting all of the dots is not the main goal. Making relationships is the main purpose. We begin by finding ways to fall in love with our creator and also with each other."

One should not assume that we are all in the same place spiritually. When we take on the role of leading a

KonXional Group we also begin to take ownership of our personal walk with God. We cannot give what we do not have. This doesn't mean that you are expected to be a spiritual giant. You are expected to be moving forward in your walk and taking seriously the scriptural commands of seeking for the Kingdom of God first.

Jeremiah 29:14 (NRSV) For surely I know the plans I have for you, says the LORD, plans for your welfare and not for harm, to give you a future with hope. Then when you call upon me and come and pray to me, I will hear you. When you search for me, you will find me; if you seek me with all your heart, I will let you find me, says the LORD, and I will restore your fortunes and gather you from all the nations and all the places where I have driven you, says the LORD, and I will bring you back to the place from which I sent you into exile.

B} Clear Direction for KonXional Groups

Each KonXional group that comes together should create a document by which they govern themselves. This Covenant should include:

Duration of KonXional Group – Each time a new group forms they are testing the ground on which they are walking. Each of the members may or may not feel comfortable to stay within this group for a long period of time. Groups must have some form of chemistry to stay together.

New KonXional Groups should commit to a short duration in which they will allow the group dynamics to form. These groups can last six to ten weeks.

Clear and Precise Purpose – Each group will at some point begin to identify its purpose for coming together. What the group becomes may not necessarily be what was originally defined. Yet, definition gives a starting place. Some groups that have a definite purpose may include an emphasis on being Missional.

I can give two distinct examples of this. I met four ladies who had an affinity for yard sales. They were extremely gifted in going to yard sales. They also had developed a desire to help the community through studying God's word in the small group setting. They began to pray for God's direction. God brought them together with a gentleman who had closed down one of his car dealerships.

They transformed this building into a Resale Boutique. When entering, you would never know that the items had been used before. They sold items at extremely low prices. Soon they discovered that after their expenses they had money to give to other groups that were looking to start up their own Outward Focused Ministry.

Another group may begin to focus on supporting others in a similar situation. Mothers of small children may come together to give emotional and physical support to their group members. They may learn that together they can conquer bigger obstacles than fighting them alone.

Other groups may simply be a group of friends that already enjoy getting together and wish to continue in a more structured meeting. This type of group may also determine the length of time that the group decides to commit too.

Group Attendance – Each member should take this Covenant seriously enough to commit to the appointed meetings and also to the time. All meetings should start on time and also end on time. If for any reason a person is going to be late or missing, they should make the call to let the group know of their situation. This is respectful action for all the members of the group.

Safe Environment – Each person must feel safe physically, emotionally, and spiritually. The only way in which this can become a reality is to be slow to make judgments (no one is there to fix another person) slow to make answers, and allow all members to be heard.

Confidentiality – Safe environments are also made by everyone being willing to keep all information confidential. Unfortunately this environment does not happen overnight. Not all people come will enter the group setting with the same level of trust or openness. At each meeting the group leader needs to regularly remind the group of the covenant of confidentiality until a shared level of trust has been established and is practiced by all.

Conflict Resolution – We must become extremely good at Jesus' instruction found in Matthew.

Matthew 18:15-17 (NRSV) "If another member of the church sins against you, go and point out the fault when the two of you are alone. If the member listens to you, you have regained that one. But if you are not listened to, take one or two others along with you, so that every word may be confirmed by the evidence of two or three witnesses. If the member refuses to listen to them, tell it to the church; and if the offender refuses to listen even to the church, let such a one be to you as a Gentile and a tax collector.

Community Member – Each person of the KonXional Group is committed to helping others go deeper in their walk with God, be willing to know others in deeper committed ways, pray for each other, and to be willing to walk with others in difficult moments.

The truth is that when a group of people come together, more than likely within one year someone will go through an experience that would be better if they had someone walk with them through it.

C} Core Requirements

Fellowship – This one topic could take in itself days. What I want to emphasize is that all we do together is fellowship. We can be very creative in what we do and where we do it. You have permission to come together in any form that is healthy for the entire KonXional Group. Let me put in a point of caution here. If one of the members struggles in a particular area, then the group will take that a signal not to open the doors to these struggles. If one is an alcoholic, don't meet in a bar to socialize. What ideas come to mind for you?

Worship – This is also an area where one can become extremely creative. I normally don't refer to the dictionary, but in this case it might not be a bad place to start.

wor·ship (wûr'shĭp) *n.*
1. a. The reverent love and devotion accorded a deity, an idol, or a sacred object. **b.** The ceremonies, prayers, or other religious forms by which this love is expressed.
2. Ardent devotion; adoration.

Worship is found in almost any activity that we perform or participate in. Our Creator formed us to have enjoyment with self and others, with a need for expression, with a desire to give, and to love. Therefore, worship can truly be utilized in all of our functions as we learn to give the functions over to God and to allow space for the blessings to flow towards heaven.

Discipleship – KonXional Groups are very similar in nature to how Jesus lived with the twelve followers. They walked, ate, worked and lived together in close proximity to learn more on the subject of loving God and Humanity. It is by coming together regularly that we are lead to trusted spiritual growth. Quality does not trump quantity.

Missional Activity – KonXional Groups grow together when they begin to place their focus on others instead of self. Members of the group become the hands and feet of Christ in their local area, regionally, and globally.

I, Stephen, personally have been on several of these types of missional trips. It is almost impossible not to become extremely bonded with the other members on the team. These bonds are not easily broken when the teams returns home.

Ministry – KonXional Groups strive to be complete in their walk with Christ. Christ commanded his disciples to go into the world to reach others with the Good News. No longer should the "Body of Christ" put stock in superficial formulaic methods: the mission is to become friends with those who are still Outside the Body.

A Bit of Caution: Balance is the key to a healthy KonXional Group. It is imperative to include regularly each of the Core Requirements, but it is just as important to place the proper emphases on each Requirement.

Your Author
Stephen Crowell

For most of Stephen's childhood he lived on what was his grandparent's farm in Western New York. The forests were his playground. At the time he loved the winter months, building ice forts and skiing on the back hill. Now though, Stephen has a hard time with the winter's cold and snow after living all over the southern states of America.

Stephen was fortunate to have served as youth and young adult pastor under his father in two different Wesleyan Churches. He then was asked to serve a small rural church in Leon, New York which is famous for their Amish community. While serving as a pastor, Stephen completed his Outdoor-Recreation degree from Houghton College. This degree came in handy when Stephen served as a camp director for the United Methodist Church in Pennsylvania.

Currently Stephen is serving as a senior pastor back in Western New York for the United Methodist Church. His passion has been working to develop an emerging church model. Stephen desires to bring people back to the radical message that Jesus taught his disciples. We have a responsibility to be in close intimate fellowship groups that help to support each other through the good and the bad.

Jesus also taught us to have an outward looking focus. Stephen understands that the message of the cross is for those who are marginalized and are sitting on the fringes. He believes that we need to break down all barriers to the foot of the cross. Another area that Stephen feels is important for the community of Christ's followers is to come together regularly to share common meals. It seems that scripture is regularly depicting Jesus eating with friends, relatives, strangers, and most importantly sinners.

Stephen is dedicated to spending any and all spare time traveling with his wife, Kristan, and with any of the kids that desire to come along. They have eight children, one of which is a daughter-in-law. They now use the excuse that the kids live in different parts of the country to visit with them. (Texas, Alaska, Florida)

If this book has helped you with your life's journey Stephen would love to hear from you. If you have a story about how this book has helped you, or changed your life, please share it with him at pastor@konxions.org .

May God bless you on your journey.
Pastor Stephen Crowell

Acknowledgements

This section could take on so many multiple pages. I promise to spare you the pain of reading through a long dissertation. I always place you, Kristan, at the top of the list, because it is through your patience with me that I dare strive to tackle these difficult projects. I know that when I get home at night my days will always be bright.

This is one project that each of my children have helped me develop. Charissa was the one who helped me understand that there needed to be an interpreter between ourselves when it came to discussions about theology. Stephen is continuously on the phone with me challenging my thought process. Seth and Brittany helped me to understand how to place people together who are far, far, far away. Justin, Jesse, Connor and Ian have lived through many of our KonXional Groups and have helped develop and set-up the Celebration Events. Thank you all for being part of the ministry.

Craig Beulow, my assistant pastor and close friend, I truly thank you for your attention to the small details. Many nights we have sat in the office and had thrown mud up against the wall to see what would stick. Not many people have the ability to work in such an environment.

Lee Capodagli has been an awesome editor on this project. He poses question upon question that bring the point I want to make into focus. I always want to "hit it hard" where Lee wants to take it slow so that he can take his time and let it effervesce. This truly is the best way so that all points get there due attention.

I want to express a gratitude for those that we serve each week. You give us the inspiration to continually move forward with the confidence of your support.

10457356R00077

Made in the USA
Charleston, SC
06 December 2011